by Iain Gray

79 Main Street, Newtongrange,
Midlothian EH22 4NA
Tel: 0131 344 0414   Fax: 0845 075 6085
E-mail: info@lang-syne.co.uk
www.langsyneshop.co.uk

Design by Dorothy Meikle
Printed by Printwell Ltd
© Lang Syne Publishers Ltd 2016

All rights reserved. No part of this publication may be reproduced, stored or introduced into a retrieval system, or transmitted in any form or by any means (electronic, mechanical, photocopying, recording or otherwise) without the prior written permission of Lang Syne Publishers Ltd.

ISBN 978-1-85217-524-5

Lee

MOTTO:
Strength with virtue.

CREST:
An erect arm with the hand
clutching a broken spear.

NAME variations include:
Lea
Legh
Leigh
Ley
Leyie

Chapter one:

The origins of popular surnames

by George Forbes and Iain Gray

If you don't know where you came from, you won't know where you're going is a frequently quoted observation and one that has a particular resonance today when there has been a marked upsurge in interest in genealogy, with increasing numbers of people curious to trace their family roots.

Main sources for genealogical research include census returns and official records of births, marriages and deaths – and the key to unlocking the detail they contain is obviously a family surname, one that has been 'inherited' and passed from generation to generation.

No matter our station in life, we all have a surname – but it was not until about the middle of the fourteenth century that the practice of being identified by a particular surname became commonly established throughout the British Isles.

Previous to this, it was normal for a person to be identified through the use of only a forename.

But as population gradually increased and there were many more people with the same forename, surnames were adopted to distinguish one person, or community, from another.

Many common English surnames are patronymic in origin, meaning they stem from the forename of one's father – with 'Johnson,' for example, indicating 'son of John.'

It was the Normans, in the wake of their eleventh century conquest of Anglo-Saxon England, a pivotal moment in the nation's history, who first brought surnames into usage – although it was a gradual process.

For the Normans, these were names initially based on the title of their estates, local villages and chateaux in France to distinguish and identify these landholdings.

Such grand descriptions also helped enhance the prestige of these warlords and generally glorify their lofty positions high above the humble serfs slaving away below in the pecking order who had only single names, often with Biblical connotations as in Pierre and Jacques.

6 *The origins of popular surnames*

The only descriptive distinctions among the peasantry concerned their occupations, like 'Pierre the swineherd' or 'Jacques the ferryman.'

Roots of surnames that came into usage in England not only included Norman-French, but also Old French, Old Norse, Old English, Middle English, German, Latin, Greek, Hebrew and the Gaelic languages of the Celts.

The Normans themselves were originally Vikings, or 'Northmen', who raided, colonised and eventually settled down around the French coastline.

The had sailed up the Seine in their longboats in 900AD under their ferocious leader Rollo and ruled the roost in north eastern France before sailing over to conquer England in 1066 under Duke William of Normandy – better known to posterity as William the Conqueror, or King William I of England.

Granted lands in the newly-conquered England, some of their descendants later acquired territories in Wales, Scotland and Ireland – taking not only their own surnames, but also the practice of adopting a surname, with them.

But it was in England where Norman rule and custom first impacted, particularly in relation to the adoption of surnames.

This is reflected in the famous *Domesday Book*, a massive survey of much of England and Wales, ordered by William I, to determine who owned what, what it was worth and therefore how much they were liable to pay in taxes to the voracious Royal Exchequer.

Completed in 1086 and now held in the National Archives in Kew, London, 'Domesday' was an Old English word meaning 'Day of Judgement.'

This was because, in the words of one contemporary chronicler, "its decisions, like those of the Last Judgement, are unalterable."

It had been a requirement of all those English landholders – from the richest to the poorest – that they identify themselves for the purposes of the survey and for future reference by means of a surname.

This is why the *Domesday Book*, although written in Latin as was the practice for several centuries with both civic and ecclesiastical records, is an invaluable source for the early appearance of a wide range of English surnames.

Several of these names were coined in connection with occupations.

These include Baker and Smith, while Cooks, Chamberlains, Constables and Porters were

8 *The origins of popular surnames*

to be found carrying out duties in large medieval households.

The church's influence can be found in names such as Bishop, Friar and Monk while the popular name of Bennett derives from the late fifth to mid-sixth century Saint Benedict, founder of the Benedictine order of monks.

The early medical profession is represented by Barber, while businessmen produced names that include Merchant and Sellers.

Down at the village watermill, the names that cropped up included Millar/Miller, Walker and Fuller, while other self-explanatory trades included Cooper, Tailor, Mason and Wright.

Even the scenery was utilised as in Moor, Hill, Wood and Forrest – while the hunt and the chase supplied names that include Hunter, Falconer, Fowler and Fox.

Colours are also a source of popular surnames, as in Black, Brown, Gray/Grey, Green and White, and would have denoted the colour of the clothing the person habitually wore or, apart from the obvious exception of 'Green', one's hair colouring or even complexion.

The surname Red developed into Reid, while

Blue was rare and no-one wanted to be associated with yellow.

Rather self-important individuals took surnames that include Goodman and Wiseman, while physical attributes crept into surnames such as Small and Little.

Many families proudly boast the heraldic device known as a Coat of Arms, as featured on our front cover.

The central motif of the Coat of Arms would originally have been what was borne on the shield of a warrior to distinguish himself from others on the battlefield.

Not featured on the Coat of Arms, but highlighted on page three, is the family motto and related crest – with the latter frequently different from the central motif.

Adding further variety to the rich cultural heritage that is represented by surnames is the appearance in recent times in lists of the 100 most common names found in England of ones that include Khan, Patel and Singh – names that have proud roots in the vast sub-continent of India.

Echoes of a far distant past can still be found in our surnames and they can be borne with pride in commemoration of our forebears.

Chapter two:

Honours and distinction

While 'Lee' is also a popular forename in modern times, as a surname it has been present in England from the earliest times.

Along with spelling variants that include 'Leigh' and 'Lea', it derives from the Old English 'leah', indicating a forest clearing or a pasture clearing, and would have originally denoted someone who worked and lived in such an area.

So common were such topographical features throughout England that to this day, in the form of 'Leigh', it lends itself to several place-names.

Wholly different derivations of the name include from the Gaelic 'laoidigh', indicating 'poet', while in recent times it has been adopted as a surname by the travelling people known as the Romanies – derived from the Romany name 'purram', meaning 'onion.'

Yet another culinary derivation of the name, found particularly among Chinese-Americans, is from 'li', indicating 'plum.'

In England, by the very nature of its derivation

from a common topographical feature, the name is found throughout the length and breadth of the country.

Also, in common with many other popular English surnames, although it did not become widespread until the decades following the Norman Conquest of 1066, bearers of what would later become the name were toiling the soil of England for a considerable period before this.

This means that flowing through the veins of many bearers of the name today may well be the blood of those Germanic tribes who invaded and settled in the south and east of the island of Britain from about the early fifth century.

Known as the Anglo-Saxons, they were composed of the Jutes, from the area of the Jutland Peninsula in modern Denmark, the Saxons from Lower Saxony, in modern Germany and the Angles from the Angeln area of Germany.

It was the Angles who gave the name 'Engla land', or 'Aengla land' – better known as 'England.'

They held sway in what became known as England from approximately 550 to 1066, with the main kingdoms those of Sussex, Wessex, Northumbria, Mercia, Kent, East Anglia and Essex.

12 *Honours and distinction*

Whoever controlled the most powerful of these kingdoms was tacitly recognised as overall 'king' – one of the most noted being Alfred the Great, King of Wessex from 871 to 899.

It was during his reign that the famous *Anglo-Saxon Chronicle* was compiled – an invaluable source of Anglo-Saxon history – while Alfred was designated in early documents as *Rex Anglorum Saxonum*, King of the English Saxons.

But the death knell of Anglo-Saxon supremacy was sounded with the Conquest of England in October of 1066, under the leadership of Duke William of Normandy.

In this pivotal event in English history, Harold II was killed at the battle of Hastings, the last of the Anglo-Saxon kings, while William was declared King of England on December 25.

What followed was the complete subjugation of his Anglo-Saxon subjects, with those Normans who had fought on his behalf – some of whom had fought at Hastings – rewarded with the lands of Anglo-Saxons, many of whom sought exile abroad as mercenaries.

While many Normans granted lands retained their original family name, others adopted the centuries-

Lee 13

old name of the territory in which they had settled – such as territories originally identified as 'Lee', 'Leigh' or 'Lea.'

One family was granted lands in Cheshire and one in Shropshire – both originally adopting the Norman-French form of 'de Lee', meaning 'of Lee.'

Within an astonishingly short space of time, Norman manners, customs and law were imposed on England – laying the basis for what subsequently became established 'English' custom and practice.

But beneath the surface, old Anglo-Saxon culture was not totally eradicated: some aspects were absorbed into those of the Normans, while faint echoes of the Anglo-Saxon past is still seen today in the form of popular names such as Lee.

Bearers of the name figure prominently in the historical record of the British Isles, with many achieving high honours and distinction.

Born in 1718, George Lee held both political and academic office while also serving as a courtier to King George III.

Acceding to the title of 3rd Earl of Lichfield in 1743 following the death of his father, he had previously served as Member of Parliament (MP) for

Oxfordshire, while in the Royal Court he held the honorary post of Lord of the Bedchamber to George III.

Also Chancellor of the University of Oxford, he died in 1772.

Not only a soldier but also a diplomat, politician and patron of the arts, Arthur Hamilton Lee was elevated to the Peerage of the United Kingdom as 1st Viscount Lee of Fareham.

Born in 1868 in Bridport, Dorset, it was after serving in a number of military postings that included British military attaché with the U.S. Army in Cuba during the 1898 Spanish-American War that he entered British politics.

Elected MP for Fareham in 1900, he served during the First World War of 1914 to 1918 in a number of Government departments that included the Ministry of Munitions; elevated to the Peerage in 1918 as Baron Lee of Fareham, of Chequers in the County of Buckinghamshire, he later served for a time as First Lord of the Admiralty.

The magnificent country house and estate of Chequers had been bought by Lee and his wife in 1912. After carrying out considerable restoration work, they gifted the house five years later to the

Lee 15

nation as an official residence and country retreat for British Prime Ministers.

As a patron of the arts, and also having been further promoted in the Peerage to the title of 1st Viscount Lee of Fareham, of Bridport in the County of Dorset, he also helped to establish the Courtauld Institute of Art in London, opened in 1932; he died in 1947.

Born in 1884 and educated at Manchester Grammar School, John Leigh was the cotton industry entrepreneur who in 1921 used part of his vast wealth to buy the *Pall Mall Gazette* newspaper.

Knighted and later elevated to the Peerage as Sir John Leigh, 1st Baronet, of Altrincham, in Cheshire, he died in 1959.

16 *Heroes and villains*

Chapter three:

Heroes and villains

It is not only on British shores that bearers of the Lee name have stamped their mark on the historical record.

One notable American family of Lees is one that traces a descent from Colonel Richard Lee, who immigrated to Virginia in 1639 and made his fortune from tobacco plantations.

It had long been held for centuries that he descended from a Lee family of Alveley, in the English county of Shropshire, but research published in 1988 by the *National Genealogical Society Quarterly Magazine* suggests that he may have been from a family in the county of Worcestershire.

But while doubt may surround his roots, what is known with certainty is that, also known as "Richard the Immigrant", he was the founder of a noted dynasty of Lees – with his descendants Francis Lightfoot Lee and Richard Henry Lee signatories in 1776 of the famous *American Declaration of Independence*.

Of the same dynasty, Henry Lee III, born in

Lee 17

1756 and who was also known by his nickname of "Light Horse Harry", served with distinction under General George Washington during the American War of Independence and as Governor of Virginia from 1791 to 1794.

He died in 1818, while one of his six children was the famed Robert Edward Lee, better known as General Robert E. Lee.

Born in 1807 at Stratford Hall Plantation in Westmoreland County, Virginia, he served during the American Civil War of 1861 to 1865 as Commander of the Confederate Army of Northern Virginia.

He is honoured in the form of an imposing statue that was erected in New Orleans fourteen years after his death in 1870.

Also on the field of battle – but not related to the Lees of Virginia – Hubert Lee was a recipient during the Korean War of the Medal of Honor, America's highest award for military valour.

Born in 1915 in Leland, Mississippi, he had been a Master Sergeant with the 23rd Infantry Regiment, 2nd Infantry Division, when in February of 1951 near Ip-Ori, Korea, he performed the actions for which he was awarded the medal.

With his platoon driven from its position

18 *Heroes and villains*

under heavy enemy fire and with the platoon leader wounded, Lee assumed command and, rallying his comrades, managed to retake the position; he died in 1982.

Back to British shores and during the Second World War, David Lee, born in 1912 in Swindon, Wiltshire, served as a pilot with No. 61 Squadron, then No. 601 Squadron, and later as Deputy Director of Plans at the War Ministry.

Serving in a number of other senior posts after the war, including Commandant of the RAF Staff College, he died in 2004 after having previously been knighted.

One Lee who made a significant contribution to the art of warfare was the Scots-Canadian, and later American, arms designer and inventor James Paris Lee.

Born in 1831 in Hawick, in the Scottish Borders and immigrating with his family at the age of five to Galt, Ontario, he was aged only twelve when he built his first gun.

The weapon failed to fire effectively, but this did not deter Lee from pursuing a career as a gunsmith.

Moving to Wisconsin, in the United States, in 1861 he developed a breech-loading cartridge conversion for the Springfield Rifled Musket.

Lee 19

Best known, however, for his development of what became the Lee-Enfield rifle, subsequently used by armies throughout the world, he died in 1904.

From the battlefield to the realms of religion, Ann Lee, better known as Mother Ann Lee, was the leader of the United Society of Believers in Christ's Second Appearing – better known as The Shakers.

Born in Manchester in 1736, she first became known, in her native England, for her fiery preaching on the Second Coming of Christ. This, she said, would only come about through confession of sins and celibacy.

Immigrating with a small group of her followers to New York in 1774, she established a small community in Albany County – becoming known as 'Shaking Quakers' or 'Shakers' by worshipping through ecstatic dancing, or 'shaking.'

She died in 1784.

In the contemporary world of invention, Sir Timothy Berners-Lee is the British computer scientist better known as Tim Berners-Lee – inventor of the World Wide Web.

Born in London in 1955, he studied from 1973 to 1976 at Queen's College, Oxford, obtaining a first-class degree in physics.

20 *Heroes and villains*

Working for a time in Poole, Dorset, as an engineer for the telecommunications company Plessey, he later joined another Dorset-based company where he was instrumental in the creation of type-setting software for printers.

Working for a period in 1980 as a consultant for CERN, an abbreviation from the French that translates as The European Organisation for Nuclear Research, and based on the Franco-Swiss border, he proposed and developed a project which would later form the basis of the World Wide Web – the concept of utilising hypertext to facilitate the sharing and updating of information among CERN researchers.

Employed from late 1980 until 1984 for a computer systems company in Bournemouth, gaining further experience in computer networking, he explored the possibilities of what was known as 'real-time remote procedure call.'

Returning to CERN, which by 1989 had the largest Internet node in Europe, Berners-Lee success-fully 'married' hypertext with the Internet – giving rise to what became the World Wide Web.

It was on August 6, 1991, that the first website, built by CERN, went online.

Berners-Lee later said: "Most of the technology

Lee   21

involved in the web, like the hypertext, like the Internet, multi-font text objects, had been designed already. I just had to put them together."

Director of the World Wide Web Consortium (W3C) charged with the oversight of the continued development of the web, he is the recipient of a host of honours and accolades.

Knighted in 2004 in recognition of his pioneering work, he is a member of the World Wide Web Hall of Fame and a Fellow of the American Academy of Arts and Sciences.

Other honours include the award in 2003 of the Royal Photographic Society's Progress Medal and Honorary Fellowship 'in recognition of any invention, research, publication or other contribution which has resulted in an important advance in the scientific or technological development of photography or imaging in the widest sense.'

Also known by his Internet user-name of 'TimBL' and holder of the Founders Chair at the MIT Computer Science and Artificial Intelligence Laboratory, he played a memorable role at the spectacular opening ceremony of the 2012 Summer Olympics in London.

This was when he 'tweeted': "This is for

everyone" – a message then instantly spelled out in lights attached to the chairs of the 80,000 spectators in the Olympic Stadium.

One particularly infamous – and also extremely lucky – bearer of the otherwise proud name of Lee was John Lee, also known as "Babbacombe Lee" and as "The Man They Couldn't Hang."

Born in 1864 in Devon, he survived no fewer than three attempts to hang him for murder.

Having served for a short period in the Royal Navy and later being imprisoned for theft on a number of occasions, he was convicted in 1885 of the murder about a year earlier of Emma Keyse, for whom he had carried out work, in her home at Babbacombe Bay, near Torquay, Devon.

Although the evidence against him was weak and circumstantial, he was sentenced to hang.

The sentence was set to be carried out at Exeter Prison on February 23, 1885, but three attempts to do so resulted in inexplicable failure.

Despite having been carefully tested beforehand by executioner James Berry, the trapdoor of the scaffold failed to open on three consecutive attempts.

The traumatic ordeal undergone by Lee was enough for the Home Secretary, Sir William Harcourt,

Lee 23

to commute the sentence to life imprisonment. Lee, after petitioning a number of successive Home Secretaries, pleading his innocence of the crime, was finally released from prison in 1907.

Following his release, he is known to have supported himself for a time by cashing in on his notoriety by giving newspaper interviews and delivering public lectures – but he disappears from the historical record by about the end of 1916.

One theory is that he died, destitute, in a workhouse at some time during the Second World War – while research carried out in recent years by the authors Mike Holgate and Ian David Waugh suggests he may have immigrated to the United States and died in 1945 in Milwaukee.

Chapter four:

On the world stage

Bearers of the Lee name and of its popular spelling variants that include Leigh, have gained international celebrity through a wide range of pursuits that include the world of entertainment.

Born in 1922 in Belgravia, London, Christopher Frank Cardandini Lee was the veteran British actor better known as **Christopher Lee**.

The son of Lieutenant-Colonel Geoffrey Trollope Lee, of the 60th King's Royal Rifle Corps, and Contessa Estelle Marie Cardandini, he is best known for his roles in a number of British *Hammer House of Horror* films.

These include the 1968 *Dracula Has Risen from the Grave*, the 1970 *Scars of Dracula* and, from 1979, *To the Devil, a Daughter*.

Knighted in 2009 for his services to drama and charity, other major film credits include the role of Lord Summerisle in the 1973 cult classic *The Wicker Man* and that of Muhammad Ali Jinnah, the founder of Pakistan, in the 1998 biopic *Jinnah*.

The recipient of the 2011 BAFTA Fellowship,

Lee 25

other noted film roles include that of Scaramanga in the 1974 James Bond film *The Man with the Golden Gun* and as Saruman in the 2001-2003 *Lord of the Rings* trilogy, he died in 2015.

In common with Christopher Lee, **Bernard Lee** is also known for his roles in films.

Born in 1908, he was the English actor famed as James Bond's superior 'M' in eleven Bond films that include the 1962 *Dr No*, the 1965 *Thunderball*, the 1971 *Diamonds Are Forever* and, lastly, the 1979 *Moonraker*. With other film credits that include the 1956 *The Battle of the River Plate* and the 1961 *Whistle Down the Wind*, he died in 1981.

Born in 1913 in Darjeeling, in what was then the Bengal Presidency of British India, the daughter of an English officer in the English Cavalry, **Vivien Leigh** was the stage name of the award-winning actress born Vivian Mary Hartley.

Married from 1940 until her divorce in 1960 to the English actor Laurence Olivier, she became Lady Olivier when her husband was knighted in 1947.

Rated by the American Film Institute as one of the greatest movie stars of all time, she won the Academy Award for Best Actress for her role of Scarlett O'Hara in the epic 1939 *Gone with the Wind*

26 *On the world stage*

and for Blanche DuBois in the 1951 *A Streetcar Named Desire*; she died in 1967.

In a much different film genre, **Bruce Lee** was the Chinese-American martial artist, actor and filmmaker born Lee Jan-Fan in 1940 to parents from Hong Kong. He became famous for his roles as an expert in martial arts in films that include the 1971 *The Big Boss* and the 1972 *The Way of the Dragon*; he died in 1973, the same year of the release of his last film, *Enter the Dragon*.

He was the father of the other noted martial arts expert and actor **Brandon Bruce Lee**, born in 1965 in Oakland, California.

With film credits that include the 1986 *Legacy of Rage* and the 1992 *Rapid Fire*, he was killed following an accidental shooting involving a malfunctioning prop firearm in 1993 while on the set of the film *The Crow*.

Born in 1927 in Merced, California, Jeanette Helen Morrison was the American actress better known by her stage name of **Janet Leigh**. Discovered by the actress Norma Shearer and signed to a film contract with MGM in 1945, her film debut came two years later in *The Romance of Rosy Ridge*.

With other notable film roles that include the

Lee   27

1960 Alfred Hitchcock thriller *Psycho*, for which she was awarded the Golden Globe Award for Best Supporting Actress and nominated for an Academy Award in that category, she was married from 1951 until 1962 to fellow actor Tony Curtis.

Appearing with him in a number of films that include the 1953 *Houdini*, she was also the author of books that include her 1984 *There Really was a Hollywood* and the 1995 *Psycho: Behind the Scenes of the Classic Thriller*.

The mother of the actresses Kelly Curtis and Jamie Lee Curtis, she appeared with the latter in films that include *The Fog* before her death in 2004.

Behind the camera lens, **Ang Lee**, born in 1954, is the Taiwanese-American film director, screenwriter and producer who is the recipient of two Academy Awards for Best Director.

These are for his 2005 *Brokeback Mountain* and, from 2012, *Life of Pi*, while other notable screen credits include his 2000 *Crouching Dragon, Hidden Tiger* – winner of an Academy Award for Best Foreign Language Film.

On British shores **Mike Leigh** is the acclaimed writer and director for both theatre and film born in 1943 in Welwyn, Hertfordshire.

28 *On the world stage*

Married from 1973 to 2001 to the actress Alison Steadman, who starred in his 1970s' television production *Abigail's Party*, major big screen credits include the 1993 *Naked*, for which he won the Best Director Award at the Cannes Film Festival.

The recipient of an OBE, he is also noted for his 1996 *Secrets and Lies*, winner of a BAFTA Award and nominated for an Academy Award, and for the 2004 *Vera Drake*.

From the stage to music, Norma Doloris Egstrom was the American jazz and popular music singer, songwriter and actress better known to her fans as **Peggy Lee**. Born in 1920 in Jamestown, North Dakota, she travelled to Los Angeles at the age of 17 to pursue a singing career and four years later joined the Benny Goodman Big Band.

She remained with the band for more than a year, having her first major hit in 1942 with *Somebody Else is Taking my Place*, followed a year later with *Why Don't You Do Right?*

Appearing in films that include the 1943 *Stage Door Canteen* and the 1952 *The Jazz Singer*, as a songwriter she composed songs for the 1955 Disney musical *The Lady and the Tramp*, while her 1969 hit *Is That All There Is?* won her a Grammy Award for Best

Lee 29

Vocal Performance. An inductee of the Songwriters Hall of Fame and the recipient of a Grammy Lifetime Achievement Award, she died in 2002.

Born in 1944 in Atlanta, Georgia, Brenda Mae Tarpley is the American pop, country music and rockabilly singer better known as **Brenda Lee**.

It was after recording at the age only 13 the song *Dynamite* that she received the nickname of "Little Miss Dynamite."

An inductee of the Rock and Roll, Country Music and Rockabilly Halls of Fame and the recipient in 2009 of the National Academy of Recording Arts and Sciences Lifetime Achievement Award, other memorable hits include her 1958 *Rockin Around the Christmas Tree* and, from 1960, *I'm Sorry*.

On British shores, and also in popular music, **Dianne Lee**, born in 1950, is the English singer who along with Lennie Peters was a member of the pop and folk duo Peters and Lee.

Enjoying a number of hits that include the 1973 *Welcome Home* and the 1975 *Somebody Done Somebody Wrong Song*, the duo also had for a time their own television show, *Meet Peters and Lee*.

In the rock music genre, **Albert Lee** is the English guitarist and composer who has played for

On the world stage

artistes and bands that include Jon Lord of Deep Purple, Head Hands and Feet, Eric Clapton and Emmylou Harris. Born in 1943 in Lingen, Herefordshire, he is known as "Mr Telecaster" because of his skill on the Telecaster guitar.

Back to American shores, **Arthur Lee** was the musician and singer born Arthur Taylor in 1945 in Memphis, Tennessee.

Best known as the frontman for the rock band Love, whose albums include the 1967 *Forever Changes* and the 1974 *Reel to Real* and also a collaborator with other artistes who include Jimi Hendrix and Bob Dylan, he died in 2006.

Born in 1953, **Geddy Lee**, born Gary Lee Weinrib, is the vocalist, bassist, keyboardist and songwriter with the Canadian rock band Rush. Formed in the late 1960s by Lee, guitarist Alex Lifeson and drummer Neil Peart, the band has enjoyed success with albums that include *A Farewell to Kings*.

All three members of the band were honoured in 1996 as Officers of the Order of Canada, while the band has also been inducted into the Rock and Roll Hall of Fame.

A founding member of the American glam metal band Mötley Crüe, **Tommy Lee** was born

Lee 31

Thomas Lee Bass in 1962 in Athens, Greece, the son of a U.S. serviceman and a Greek mother.

As the drummer with the band, he has enjoyed international success with albums that include the 1981 *Too Fast for Love* and the 1989 *Dr Feelgood*, while he has previously been married to the actresses Pamela Anderson and Heather Lockyear and the model Elaine Bergen.

From music to the sciences, **David Morris Lee**, born in 1931 in Rye, New York, is the physicist who shared the Nobel Prize in Physics with Robert C. Richardson and Douglas Osheroff for their work on the properties of Helium-3.

Bearers of the Lee name have also excelled in the highly competitive world of sport.

On the cricket pitch, **Brett Lee**, born in 1976, is the Australian former cricketer recognised as having been one of the fastest bowlers in the history of the game.

On the fields of European football, **Alan Lee**, born in Galway in 1978, is the Irish footballer who, in addition to playing for teams that include Aston Villa, Cardiff City and Huddersfield Town, won 10 caps playing for the Republic of Ireland between 2003 and 2006.

From sport to the world of literature, one particularly notable bearer of the proud name of Lee was Nelle Harper Lee, better known as **Harper Lee**.

Born in 1926 in Monroeville, Alabama, she is known for her 1961 Pulitzer Prize-winning novel *To Kill a Mockingbird* and, published less than a year before her death in 2016, *Go Set a Watchman*.

The novel, dealing with issues of racism that she observed while growing up in her hometown, *To Kill a Mockingbird* was adapted for a film of the same name in 1962 – winning actor Gregory Peck an Academy Award for Best Actor for his portrayal of the character Atticus Finch.

The recipient in 2007 of the Presidential Medal of Freedom, she once famously said: "In an abundant society where people have laptops, cell phones, iPods and minds like empty rooms, I still plod along with books."

As a child, she was a neighbour and school friend of the equally noted American author Truman Capote, later helping him with his research for his 1966 book dealing with a true murder case, *In Cold Blood*.

She was also portrayed by Catherine Keeper in the 2005 film *Capote* and by Sandra Bullock in the 2006 *Infamous*.